GREAT SONGS OF WORLD WAR II

with

The Home Front in Pictures

Written and edited by Michael Leitch

Book designed by David Pocknell

Picture research by Penelope Brown

Cover designed by Pearce Marchbank

Wise Publications London/New York/Sydney
Exclusive distributors to the music trade
Music Sales Ltd
8/9 Frith Street, London W1V 5TZ, England

Music Sales PTY Limited
120 Rothschild Avenue, Rosebery,
NSW 2018, Australia

CONTENTS

INTRODUCTION

The songs of World War II were about optimism. They needed to be, for World War II was harder on the non-fighting people of Britain than any previous war. In those harsh years the power of music in general, and popular songs in particular, to distract and encourage a people quite unused to living under siege conditions was doubly valuable – for national morale as well as for the timeless, 'play-it-again' feeling that every good song can give to its listeners.

The hardships of the war were numerous. Even so, many of them were not wholly unexpected. The Great War of 1914-18 had already shown, by naval blockade and primitive aerial attack, that warfare in the 20th century was destined to be a total business, something that could not be settled by armies fighting in isolation.

By the late '30s, as the nations of Europe drifted apart, it became impossible not to 'think war'. Men volunteered to join or were conscripted into the armed forces. Women joined auxiliary services such as the ATS or the Women's Land Army. All left home and loved ones behind, exchanging everyday jobs for a doubtful future.

As for the others, the stay-at-homes, they were perhaps still more unfortunate. They found themselves landed, as the war arrived and gathered momentum, with a fourth-rate version of their normal peace-time lives – blacked out, bombed out, queuing for everything. What was more, they were also being asked to fight, or at least actively resist, the enemy – by joining the ARP, the LDV, the WVS, and so on. For the better educated, the middle classes, it was easier to respond to such calls. Millions of less fortunate people found them mystifying, threatening. The notion of Them and Us was strongly felt. A Government slogan which said 'Your Courage, Your Cheerfulness, Your Resolution Will Bring Us Victory' provoked many an anti-Establishment raspberry. This is not to belittle the courage and patriotism shown by all social ranks: it was simply that some people in the '30s had been having a hard enough time without the added obligations of a war; and they needed longer to get used to them.

Some of the mystification arose from the immense weight of strange equipment that people found themselves acquiring. For this, the planners insisted and from experience none could refute them – this was to be the bomber's war; civilian populations would be pounded as never before until one side capitulated. So it was not seen as madness when, in September 1938, 38 million gas masks were handed round. After all, the newsreels showed that Hitler's Kondor Legion was getting better and better at hitting Republican targets in Spain. Would we be next?

Of course, once you had a gas mask you had to carry it about with you; you needed a case to put it in. Then along came an Anderson shelter to crouch in. The rhythms of war took over. The bombers were coming so black out your windows and send your children off to the countryside, while your husband/son/lover/brother went to France/the Atlantic/the Far East/up in the air.

WILLS'S CIGARETTES

THE CIVILIAN DUTY RESPIRATOR

Inseparable from this melodramatic flood of surprises and intimations of disaster, soon to be followed by real ones, was the music of the war– above all, the songs. Wherever they were sung – in dance halls, on the radio, in the factories – they gave men and women a few minutes' oblivion, a laugh, the heart to carry on. Whatever happens, was their constant message, we'll meet again, have a barrel of fun, a lovely week-end, nightingales will sing in Berkeley Square, we'll gather lilacs, get lit-up; so praise the Lord and pass the ammunition. And, their emotions heightened by the war, people listened closely to the words, found them moving, even beautiful, guffawed, wept, needed to believe them.

The songs of World War II were, as we said before, about optimism. The Government saw to it that they were. In Hitler's war it was all or nothing. From their bases in Germany Lord Haw Haw's brigade of enemy propagandists was giving the Ministry of Information headaches enough, and songs having even a remotely defeatist content were not permitted. This battle began before the war, the Lord Chamberlain banning jokes and songs about Hitler as far back as 1936 when a song, *Even Hitler had a Mother*, was blue-pencilled. Once war had begun, the ban was lifted; but the spirit behind it remained. A consequence seems to have been that relatively few songs 'knocking' the enemy became popular.

For every special emotion of wartime there was at least one special song. For patriotism, what better symbol could there have been than *There'll always be an England*? Among the numerous songs of love and parting perhaps *We'll meet again*, *Yours* and *Lilli Marlene* were supreme. The comedies of service life, the daunting smells of the cookhouse linger still in *Kiss me goodnight, Sergeant-major* and *In the Quartermaster's Stores*. Rationing produced its own crop of food songs, among them *Run, rabbit, run!* and *Hey! Little Hen!* Finally, there were the countless songs of good cheer, *You are my Sunshine*, *Bless 'em all*, *Roll out the Barrel* and the song that stood for the end – and victory – *I'm going to get lit-up, when the Lights go up in London*.

In the pages that follow the course of everyday events on the Home Front is traced from the first deep rumblings of danger in 1938 to the Victory parties of 1945. Many of the songs that appear in the *Music Section* are picked out and placed in their historical context. The aim is to show something of what it was like to be alive in those years when the British, accepting that war was no knees-up, responded nonetheless to the call:

Everybody do the 'Blackout Stroll'
Laugh and drive your cares right up the pole.

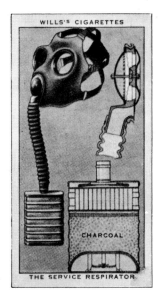

WILLS'S CIGARETTES

CHARCOAL

THE SERVICE RESPIRATOR

THE BUILD-UP TO WAR

1919: 28 June
Treaty of Versailles signed, officially ending World War I but inflicting deep humiliation on German people through disarmament, confiscation of territories and excessive bill for reparations.

1930: 14 September
Hitler's National Socialists (Nazis) emerge as major party in Reichstag elections.

1933: 30 January
Adolf Hitler becomes German Chancellor.

1935: 16 March
Hitler abolishes military restraints of Versailles Treaty and orders conscription for his new and enlarged armed forces.

1936: 7 March
German troops reoccupy Rhineland.

1938: 13 March
Hitler annexes Austria. 'Greater Germany' is born.

May
Hitler's plans to take over Czechoslovakia, beginning with Sudetenland, meet resistance from Britain, France and Russia. Relations with Germany worsen.

25 September
War seems near. In Britain ARP services are mobilized, trenches dug, barrage balloons launched, 38 million gas masks issued.

29 September
Anglo-German concord signed in Munich.

1939: 15 March
German troops enter Prague.

17 March
Britain and France protest against violation of Munich agreement.

28 April
British Parliament votes in conscription.

22 May
Hitler and Mussolini sign Pact of Steel.

23 August
Russo-German pact signed in Moscow.

1 September
Germans invade Poland.

1-3 September
In Britain, blackouts begin in earnest; mass evacuation started to countryside.

3 September
Britain and France declare war on Germany.

September 1938: the call goes out for women to join the newly formed ATS – and so free a man for combat duties in the event of war.

By February 1938, long before Britain declared war, Hitler's expansionist aims in Europe had made a clash of arms seem likely. Seen here is a recruiting post for the Territorial Army.

BLIMEY!

In a Penguin Special published in November 1939 and entitled *Why Britain is at War*, Harold Nicolson wrote of the British: 'This sleepy, decent and most pacific race can only be roused to violent action by two emotions: the first is fear; the second is anger. Before he agrees to make war the Briton must have (a) a sense of personal danger and (b) a sense of personal outrage.'

After March 1939, when the Germans marched into Prague, the real danger to Britain of Hitler's lust for territorial gain was clear to see. Britons were no longer so somnolent: there was anger at the Munich betrayal as well as horror at the treatment of the Czechs. Most now seemed to agree that war had become more a matter of 'when' than 'if'. All the same, if there was also a trace of unwillingness to fight, even despair at the prospect, this too was hardly surprising. A nation that had lost almost a million subjects in the Great War, and suffered a further two million wounded, was being asked, barely twenty years later, to do it all over again. Blimey!

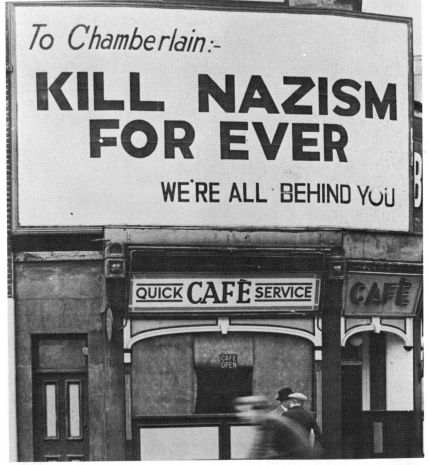

A 'Get Hitler' poster that conveys the exasperation as well as the anger felt by many observers of the Nazi menace.

Newspaper bill-boards reveal the latest stages in the drift towards war.

In April 1939 Parliament decided that patriotism alone was not enough, and conscription was started. It was the first peacetime enforcement of military service in British history. At first it applied only to men aged 20-21, but as soon as war was declared all men between 18 and 41 became liable for call-up.

Newspaper bill-boards, some more accurate than others announce, the arrival of conscription (in fact for men aged 20-21).

Within months the Army's clothing factories were hard-pressed to equip the flood of conscripts. The photo shows machinists at work on greatcoats for the approaching winter.

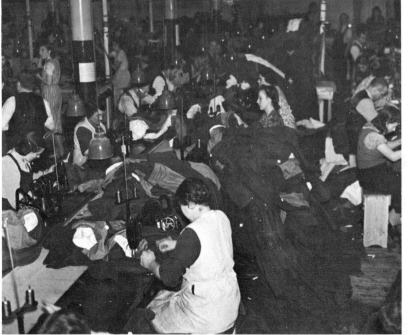

Opposite:
Britannia leads the call to arms.

DAD'S ARMY

Resisting attack from the air and invasion by sea were the top priorities with the Civil Defence organizations. The ARP (Air Raid Precautions) was formed in April 1937 and got seriously down to work in September 1938. In April 1940, Anthony Eden, then Secretary of State for War, launched a new arm, the LDV (Local Defence Volunteers), later known as the Home Guard; this was open to men between 17 and 65 who had not been called up but wanted to take an active part in the war effort.

Home Guards learn to operate a machine gun.

Employees of the LNER, in their part-time role as Local Defence Volunteers, prepare to defend their lines.

ARP

CALLING YOU

GET INTO TOUCH WITH YOUR LOCAL COUNCIL

WILLS'S CIGARETTES

ARP

AIR RAID PRECAUTIONS BADGE

A pub-style sign outside an ARP post in Wembley.

Men of the Auxiliary Fire Service on parade.

TAKING SHELTER

At the time of the Munich crisis trenches were dug in parks and barrage balloons ('blimps') floated over London. Anderson shelters, named after Sir John Anderson, later Minister of Home Security, were issued early in 1939 to those with gardens to put them in. Sandbags were in great demand for protecting buildings and creating strongpoints from which to fire on the invader – if he came.

Children fill sandbags during the first weekend of the war.

Close-up of a barrage balloon. 'It puts you in mind of a big whale,' a man told a Mass Observation researcher. Exactly what the balloons did aroused much speculation. One onlooker decided that barrages were electrified and drew enemy planes like a magnet; bombs were similarly attracted to the mooring wires and then slithered harmlessly to earth.

February 1939: housewives in Islington try out their newly delivered Anderson shelters.

September 1939: digging trenches in a London street.

NOSEBAGS

Other nicknames for the ubiquitous gas mask were dicky-bird and canary; in Barrow-in-Furness a small boy was reported to have been found crying because he had 'forgotten his 'Itler'. Their issue in September 1938 had a pronounced effect on attitudes as well as appearances: many more recruits joined the ARP, and by the outbreak of war people had had plenty of time to get used to carrying them wherever they went.

Rehearsals at a decontamination centre for gas victims: the drill was to remove your outer garments – which were put in the bins – and you were then led off for further cleansing.

Opposite:
Babies were an awkward shape for gas masks, and had to be fitted with a still more grotesque-looking helmet; this had a carrying handle at the top.

August 1939: children on their way to school, equipped for a trial evacuation. The cardboard boxes used to hold gas masks stimulated lots of jokes. People said, 'You've got your Easter Egg, I see.'

A Gloucestershire policeman wearing his respirator and a placard reminding others to do the same.

Showgirls, too, had a way of persuading people to wear their gas masks.

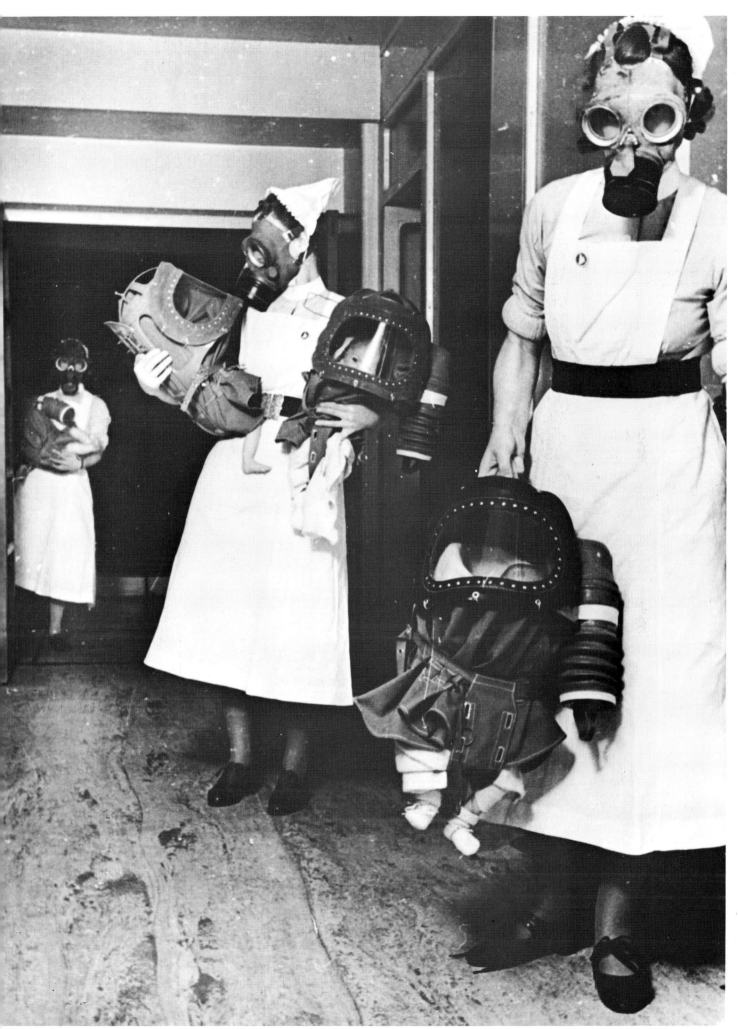

BLACKING OUT

The blackout was a chilling experience, frightening many to the extent that they no longer went out at night. It was officially introduced on 1 September 1939, the day the Germans invaded Poland, its purpose being to make the outlines of towns as vague as possible from the air. Transport workers were in effect in the front line of the blackout, and their comments are especially apt. Not a few were highly resentful, like the London bus conductor who told a Mass Observation researcher, 'I never answer people at night – I'm afraid of what I might say. It's giving me the rats properly, this blackout.' Perhaps the experience of a South Croydon porter best sums up the dangers and the other-worldliness of blackout life: 'I fell off the platform last night. Clean over the edge I fell. Thought I had turned far enough left and I hadn't. Mind you, there was a fog at the time.'

As befitted something so universally unpleasant, lots of blackout songs were written to cheer people up. In addition to the *Blackout Stroll*, mentioned earlier, there was *Crash! Bang! I want to go home*, *Follow the white line* and *They can't blackout the Moon*. Another, borrowing the tune of the *Lambeth Walk*, included this verse:

> *Down the inky avenue,*
> *Inky, pinky, parlez-vous,*
> *You'll find your way,*
> *Doing the 'Blackout Walk', Oi!*

Girls of the Worthing 'Blackout Corps' paint over the windows of a local hospital.

Opposite, above left: Students at Preston Technical College sew blackout curtains from cloth woven in the College's own Weaving Department.
Above right: A warning sign stencilled on the pavement in Southgate as part of an effort to cut down on pedestrian collisions.
Below: White-painted sticks were a popular aid for night walkers.

'GOODNIGHT CHILDREN, EVERYWHERE'

Said a landlady from Blackpool of her charges: 'They carved their initials on the sideboard. Wrote all over the wall. Ate their food on the floor. Broke half the china.' A nightmarish picture. They, of course, were not a band of literate gorillas, escaped from some zoo, but a batch of the young evacuees who came pouring out of London, some with mothers, many more without, to find refuge in the provinces from the German bombs that were daily expected after Hitler's invasion of Poland. It was a migration that appealed to very few involved in it, neither to the evacuees nor their hosts. Social classes and customs bumped rudely into one another and nobody felt like saying 'Pardon'. A letter from an evacuee mother expresses the shock of it all. Unpunctuated, it reads:

Dear Mrs —,
I am writing to let you know I have left D— and am at my sisters I couldn't stick it any longer we were treated as bits of dirt by the locals as though it wasn't bad enough going through what we did to get there we started out at eleven o'clock and didn't get to D— until 5 after five changes by train and bus and standing out on the curb in L— for an hour and twenty minutes we arrived at the skating rink and then were picked out so you can guess what some poor devils were like who had four or five children they were still there on the Sunday afternoon . . .

When Hitler's bombers did not arrive, and the 'Bore War' period set in, many evacuees drifted back home. Later, in the Blitz, came re-evacuation and also evacuation from other cities as the German bombing programme was extended.
For those who could bear to listen there was a song, *Goodnight Children, everywhere*, which was intended to link and comfort parents and children whom evacuation had separated. A correspondent recalls: 'I don't think it was heard for very long, because it upset so many parents.'

Evacuees and their teacher settle down to dormitory life in the country.

A mother sits at home in Greenwich with her youngest child and reads a letter from her four other children, now in the West Country.

Labelled children board a train at Ealing.

Apples from the Red Cross lady for new arrivals in Devon.

IT'S WAR!

Two days after Hitler's invasion of Poland, Britain declared war on Germany. The announcement was made at 11 o'clock. Minutes later air raid sirens wailed over London; soon after came the first 'All Clear'. A long period of waiting began – the 'Bore' or 'Phoney' War – which lasted until the Panzers crossed the Meuse in May 1940. Amid the blackouts, the evacuations and the many other abnormalities of wartime, patriotic feeling remained strong: *There'll always be an England* went to the top of the best-selling list in November (200,000 copies at 1s 0d each).

3 September 1939: the news comes through.

On the first day of the war a cycling policeman rides past the bus terminus at Crystal Palace with a 'Take Cover' sandwich board.

Opposite:
Soldiers outside Charing Cross station read all about it.

KEEP YOUR PECKER UP

It was a quiet autumn in Britain. The war at sea gathered pace as the Germans attacked Allied shipping with U-boats and magnetic mines. In Uruguay the *Graf Spee*, a German pocket battleship, was cornered by the Royal Navy and scuttled by her captain. In the absence of fighting nearer home, the Government kept up a propaganda war with posters and constant reminders to people to remain prepared.

The poster that caused a bitter outcry from the many who resented its Them and Us implications.

October 1939: an open-air concert, put on to keep idle troops amused.

Opposite, above: Christmas puds a-plenty in the first winter of the war.
Below:
More food for the mind – a Government slogan presses for greater unity in the war effort.

'WE'LL MEET AGAIN'

The first divisions of the Army (British Expeditionary Force) joined the Allied line at Lille in mid-October. So began five and a half years of station and dockside farewells and leavetime reunions. Scores of songs explored the theme of separation, for example *I'll pray for you*, *I'll be seeing you* and *The White Cliffs of Dover* – though none is so well remembered as *We'll meet again*, usually as sung by Vera Lynn.

A correspondent recalls: 'I was waiting on Dartford station with my little daughter, aged 4. It was in the blackout and spirits were low when without prompting she sang the chorus of *We'll meet again* right through in the darkness. When she stopped singing a naval officer standing near said "Bless her – let's hope she'll always be free to sing".'

The song was adopted by one engaged couple, and the fiancée always used the words of the title to sign off his letters from Singapore. Taken prisoner by the Japanese in 1941, he vanished for four years but survived. On his return to England he cabled his fiancée. She rushed to meet him but her train was late and she missed the last bus from the station. A sympathetic airman gave her a lift and they chased and caught the bus. Her fiancée, who had despaired of waiting for her at the station, was on board, and so they were reunited 'before a ready-made audience. But our song had come true for us and that was all that mattered!'

Time to go now.

A newly married couple leave their parish church in Bermondsey in October 1939; that autumn the threat of separation brought a flush of weddings.

A kiss of farewell after Christmas leave, 1939.

Our Vera.

Overleaf:
A vicar says goodbye to his son.

S.W.A.L.K.

Love fell into the hands of the censor. Space was limited, too, but messages like 'S.W.A.L.K.' (Sealed With A Loving Kiss) usually got through to their destination.

The Army post office at Cherbourg, in the early months of the war.

A soldier writes home from a bed of French straw.

While wives and sweethearts stayed at home in Britain, a generation of ex-civilians was beginning to appreciate the quirks of service life, and a salvo of comic songs arrived to celebrate this new vein of common experience: among them were *Kiss me goodnight, Sergeant-major*, *Nursie! Nursie!* and *In the Quartermaster's stores*.

With a fag and a grin – his is the face of optimism; he's one of the men who's going to 'hang out the washing on the Siegfried Line'.

Messing with the local population – while keeping a machine gun trained at the skies.

Royal Inniskilling Fusiliers disembark at Cherbourg.

'With his little ukelele . . .'

Nurses, newly arrived in France, unpack and check their stores.

THE WAY TO DUNKIRK

One of the most misguidedly optimistic songs of the war was *We're gonna hang out the washing on the Siegfried Line*, which was written some months before the Allies' defeat in Europe. In one sense, though, it was a great success: its cocky assertions about the future of Hitler's most strongly fortified defence line infuriated the Nazi press machine. On 6 October 1939 the *Daily Telegraph* was happy to reveal the Germans' angry reaction to a claim that the song had been written by the men of a British anti-aircraft unit. 'This is not a soldiers' song, because soldiers do not brag,' railed the German radio. 'It was not written in the soldiers' camps, but by the Jewish scribes of the BBC.' Later the Germans sought to turn the inactivity of the Phoney War to their advantage; on 30 October the *Daily Telegraph* reported a further sweeping statement:

NAZIS JEER AT BRITISH SONG
NO WASHING YET ON SIEGFRIED LINE
TOMMIES ARE ALL IN PARIS

As it turned out, a piece of washing *was* hung symbolically on the Siegfried Line – but that was in 1945, during the final Allied advance. In the meantime the rude shocks of Blitzkrieg, and the retreat to Dunkirk, lay in wait.

The words of Hitler's least favourite song are unfurled in a London night club.

A German rail gun answer back in the campaign of May-June 1940.

British troops queue to be taken off the beaches at Dunkirk.

Defeated but saved for another day – the returning army is welcomed home.

WILL THE SEA LION STRIKE?

After Dunkirk came a time of waiting. A German invasion plan, Operation Sea Lion, was prepared. Around Britain further strongpoints were set up and possible landing grounds were strewn with heavy obstacles. A Ministry of Information poster offered reassurance of a kind: 'What do I do if I hear news that Germans are trying to land, or have landed? I remember that this is the moment to act like a soldier. I do *not* get panicky. I *stay put*. I say to myself: Our chaps will deal with them . . .' But would they? The critical moment was near.

1 July 1940: Goering (fifth from right) and his staff study the coast of Britain from across the Channel.
Opposite:
Searchlight and anti-aircraft batteries keep a permanent look-out.

At first heavy roadblocks were set up, then many were removed in order not to hinder the movements of British troops.

A pile of signposts, pulled up to deny information to an invader

25 June 1940: the French stop fighting on all fronts.

Under the Emergency Powers Act censorship was applied to the press and to overseas mail; telephone trunk lines were tapped. Shown here is an office of the Postal Censorship Department.

If you've news of our munitions
KEEP IT DARK
Ships or planes or troop positions
KEEP IT DARK
Lives are lost through conversation
Here's a tip for the duration
When you've private information
KEEP IT DARK!

A striking anti-gossip poster put out by the Ministry of Information. Altogether some 2,500,000 posters were distributed during the early months of 1940.

As Fortress Britain awaited attack, moods within the nation oscillated between the defiance of Low's soldier glaring out from a rocky shore ('Very well, alone!') and the agonies of near-panic. Spies, agents, parachutists were reported everywhere. It was a time when people were inclined to listen with special care to the frightening announcements of Lord Haw-Haw ('Jairmany calling'). A. P. Herbert was more consoling:

> *Do not believe the tale the milkman tells;*
> *No troops have mutinied at Potters Bar.*
> *Nor are there submarines at Tunbridge Wells.*
> *The BBC will warn us when there are.*

Bruce Bairnsfather's poster was one of a flood reminding the nation to hold its tongue. Another cartoonist, Fougasse, produced a series using the slogan 'Careless Talk Costs Lives', in several of which the uniformed figures of Hitler and Goering were featured in attitudes of casual espionage, perching for example on luggage racks in a train, or leaning round a telephone box or sitting behind two women on a bus, smugly savouring the confidences that fell to their ears.

Now everyone had a number as well as a name. By the end of September 1939 a National Register had been drawn up and identity cards (buff coloured) were issued.

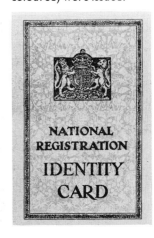

35

SAUCEPANS TO SPITFIRES

After Dunkirk there was a great surge in aircraft production, and the monthly figure for fighters, 256 in April, was almost doubled by July (496). In that month came the first raids of the Battle of Britain; in that month, too, the flamboyant Minister for Aircraft Production, Lord Beaverbrook, gave new impetus to the scrap-metal campaign of the previous government. Through the WVS he asked the women of Britain for 'everything that they can possibly give to be made into aeroplanes – Spitfires, Hurricanes, Blenheims and Wellingtons'. Although much of the national kitchenware was only distantly related to the high-grade aluminium that went into the production of Spitfires, there was an immense response and morale rose alongside the mountains of metal.

The Lambeth Walk Spitfire Fund. Many towns and other groups clubbed together to 'buy' a warplane. Spitfires were the most popular, and someone even worked out a graduated price list for smaller contributions. For 6d you could 'buy' a rivet; small bomb was £22, a Spitfire wing cost £2,000.

Herbert Morrison, Minister of Supply in the Churchill Government, was responsible for salvage operations and for providing, as he put it, 'everything from army blankets to AA guns and tanks'. His slogan was 'Go to it'.

Casting aside her mangle –
housewife responds to the
scrap-metal appeal
launched by the
Chamberlain regime. Gates
and railings were other
favoured offerings.

July 1940: workers sift
through the pots and pans
at an Aircraft Production
Dump near London.

When German bombs began to fall the nightly destruction, the fires, the deaths all seemed to more than justify those fears first aroused over twenty years before by the primitive air raids of World War I. Now every sunrise uncovered hideous changes in the landscape.

Opposite, above:
An armed Home Guard in the East End of London watches over the possessions of a bombed-out family.

Below:
Death of a city centre. The shattering of Coventry, first set on fire by incendiaries and then bombed for ten hours, marked the first concentrated bombing of a major strategic target in the provinces. It was the kind of all-out attack that later was amplified over Hamburg, Dresden and, ultimately, Hiroshima.

September 1940: the King and Queen, touring a devastated part of West London, bring comfort of a special, much-valued kind.

There were plenty of jokes about Anderson shelters. ' We're thinking of taking a lodger,' one Mass Observation researcher was told. Others resented uprooting themselves and their children from warm beds indoors. Many shelters leaked or flooded. Eventually an indoor type, the Morrison shelter, was introduced: this was a heavy steel table covered at the sides with wire mesh.

'LORDS OF THE AIR'

By spring 1941 the words of the song were seen to be true beyond doubt. The Luftwaffe had failed to crush the RAF, and as the pressure on the Home Front was gradually eased Britain's military planners prepared to move over to the offensive.

An RAF station commander briefs his air crews before a mission.

Pilots of a Spitfire squadron await the command to 'scramble'. Below: the long sprint out to the planes.

BUSINESS AS USUAL

To stay open – that was the challenge in the make-do-and-mend years of 1940 and after. Even if, like one chemist in Southampton, you felt obliged to post a notice listing all the goods that were unavailable. In March 1941 he regretted that he could not supply 'Vacuum flasks, Saccharines, Lipsticks, Rouges, All tubes of vanishing cream, All barley sugar sweets, Rolls razors, Rolls razor blades, Gillette razor blades, 7 o'clock razor blades, Brushless shaving cream, Nivea cream – UNTIL NOTICE REMOVED.'

At the improvised Dolphin, in Coventry, the beer flowed on – with stout for the ladies.

Christmas 1940 in an Anderson shelter (celebrated by this family two days early because the husband was down for all-day duty on the 25th).

Overleaf, above left: At T. Vasco's West End salon they moved the driers to an underground shelter and carried on.
Above right: Newsvendors at their pitch during a tear-gas exercise in the City of London. Because of a paper shortage newspaper sellers either wrote their own bill-boards or re-used the old familiar ones.
Below: Tea and sandbags on a sunny afternoon – what could be more reassuring?

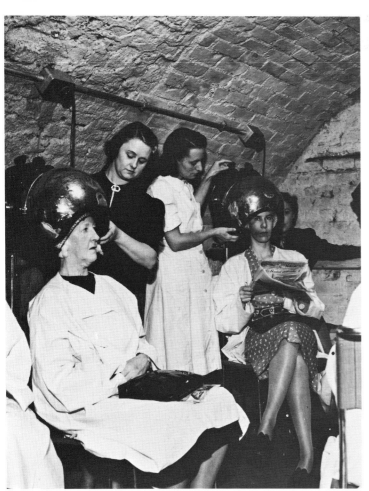

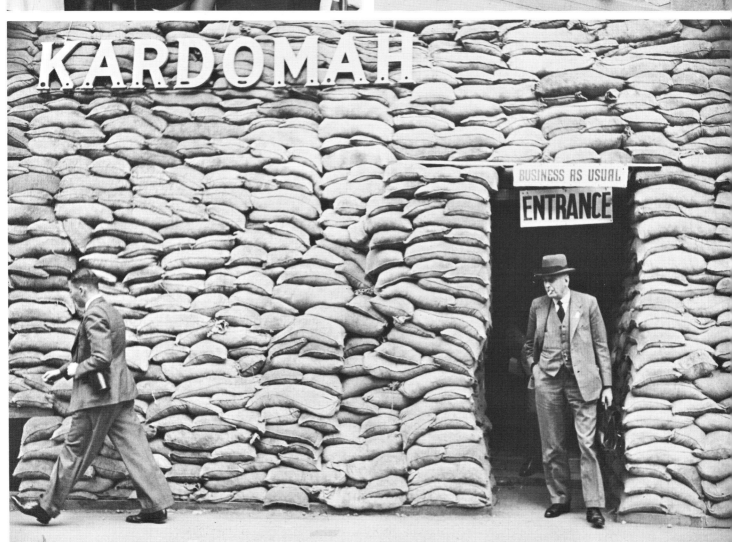

FORTUNES OF WAR

The war turned the unexpected into a daily event. A song, *Mr Brown of London Town*, catches something of the general bewilderment:

> *Things blew up and things blew down,*
> *Seemed a blinkin' shame,*
> *Bloomin' fire and flame,*
> *Blimey, what a game!*

An old man sits dumbfounded in the rubble. He had gone out for a walk with his dog one Sunday lunchtime; when he returned, his house had been bombed.

The WVS, founded in 1938 with five members, had attracted almost a million by 1941; its mobile canteens brought an oasis to many a bomb-gutted street.

Knitting went on everywhere. In the pub where this photo was taken, the landlady made a habit of asking her customers to do a few rows, as they drank, for soldiers or evacuee children.

Even remote districts were showered with the wreckage of war – in this instance German wreckage, so thumbs up all round.

DOWN THE TUBES

It all began in 1940 when Londoners rebelled against the inadequacies of public air-raid shelters and took to the Underground. Ignoring an official ban, they bought 1½d tickets, descended to the platforms and stayed there till morning.

An overspill of uneasy sleepers at Piccadilly.

Opposite: Eventually came official recognition, and with it a few positive benefits such as bunks and bucket lavatories. In this scene the night-dwellers of Aldwych station are entertained by an ENSA concert party.

Once it had arrived, rationing remained for the duration. The Ministry of Food introduced its restrictions gradually, beginning in January 1940 with bacon or ham (4 oz per head per week), butter (4 oz) and sugar (12 oz). Meat (1s 10d worth) followed in March, and tea (2 oz) in July.

The heady days of 1940, when such exotica as bananas were still on open sale, and oranges still found a way across 'Musso's Lake'.

On the Kitchen Front: a mother of sixteen settles down with a quill to her weekly calculations.

Opposite:
Counting her coupons as she leaves the shop, with a cargo of . . . what? Perhaps some of those wartime specials – Spam, dried egg or dried milk, or maybe a pound of those sausages so heavy with bread that one woman remembers, 'We didn't know whether to put mustard or marmalade on them'.

EATING OUT

To help out on the Kitchen Front, the Government stepped up the number of school meals, encouraged factories to start canteens and launched the British Restaurant, a kind of cheap cafeteria. In this way people could get a main meal *and* stay away from their larders.

Various types of communal feeding centre were started. Here an evacuee from Millwall poses at a centre in the Cotswolds with her 3d dinner.

September 1940: not a gas showroom any more but an experimental take-away feeding centre in Bradford. People brought their own bowl, jug or plate to be filled and then dashed off home before the food went cold.

DIG FOR VICTORY

The campaign to grow more food quickened as the Battle of the Atlantic cut supplies. Restrictions were raised on the keeping of poultry and rabbits in domestic gardens and these animals, together with the less common pig, duck, goat and hive of bees, enlivened many a household.

Onions, parsnips and beans flourish on the roof of a Tottenham grower's Anderson shelter.

An army allotment party prepares to move off. Note wheelbarrow smartly held in raised position.

Opposite:
In April 1941 the turf of
Kensington Gardens was
turned over and allotments
were started.

At the Tower of London,
this was arguably the
moat's finest hour.

Rashers for rozzers –
anticipatory grins at one of
the many pig clubs founded
in the war to make the
weekly meat ration go a
little further.

Those who, in contrast,
kept poultry, had a song
to aid their expectations
– *Hey, little Hen!* – with
its plea:

'Get into your nest,
Do your little best,
Get it off your chest,
I can do the rest,
Hey, little Hen!
When, when, when will
you lay me an egg
for my tea?'

DIG FOR
VICTORY

DRESSING DOWN

These were the days of black-out slacks, butter-muslin bras and blanket coats. Clothes were put on points rationing in June 1941, mainly in order to free workers in the garment industry for more urgent war work.

Should women wear trousers? Much nonsense was talked about loss of femininity, etc., when women in their thousands were already wearing them, along with other items of 'blitz wear', in factories and on farms.

Utility rayon dress – yours for 7 coupons (plus cash). The Utility scheme standardized designs, and made for long, economic production runs as well as a guaranteed product at prices within most people's reach.

The wide-shouldered, short-skirted style that lasted through the war years.

Utility unmentionables. Some of the prices of items on parade here were: matron's wool vest, 4s 2½d and 3 coupons; 11-year-old girl's vest, 4s 2½d and 2 coupons; four-year-old girl's vest, 3s 6½d and 1 coupon.

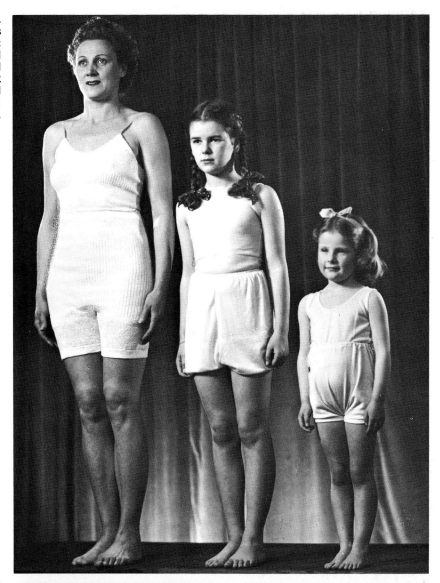

'Never throw away an old corset' sounds like the beginning of a Tommy Handley joke; it was in fact a line in a wartime Board of Trade leaflet. Women were constantly implored to 'make do and mend', and the Government devised a cartoon figure, Mrs Sew and Sew, to explain various ways of patching up and converting clothes from existing wardrobes.

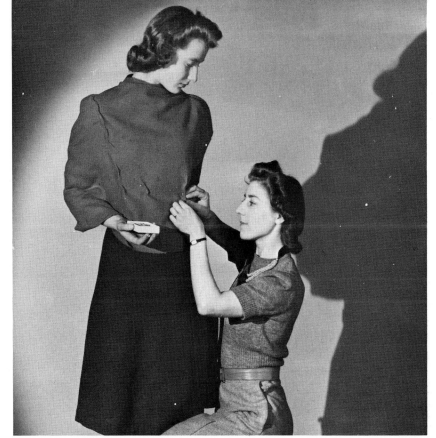

Looking back to brighter days – an Easter bonnet for 1940.

CULTURE FOR ALL

Concerts, plays and variety shows, featuring stars like Sybil Thorndike and George Formby, were staged by ENSA (Entertainments National Service Association) in factories, art galleries, churches and halls throughout the land. Some acts were too highbrow for their audiences – an out-of-place string quartet might be barracked and/or deserted – but by and large the performers brought change and sometimes a sprinkling of glamour to the humdrum routines of wartime.

Arriving at the garrison theatre for an ENSA show.

Sandwich lunches in the hall of the British Museum.

Opposite, above:
A Canadian military band plays in Trafalgar Square on Empire Day 1941.
Below:
A Southern Railway works band in rehearsal.

I s your journey really necessary? demanded the posters. If so, you wouldn't find it easy. The blackout, coupled with the absence of signposts, turned many long journeys into mystery tours.

Gas-bag power promised an early answer to the petrol shortage, but such vehicles could rarely travel more than twenty miles without a refill; despite later improved systems, gas cars were troublesome and never really caught on.

By lorry to work: commuters disembark at Blackfriars.

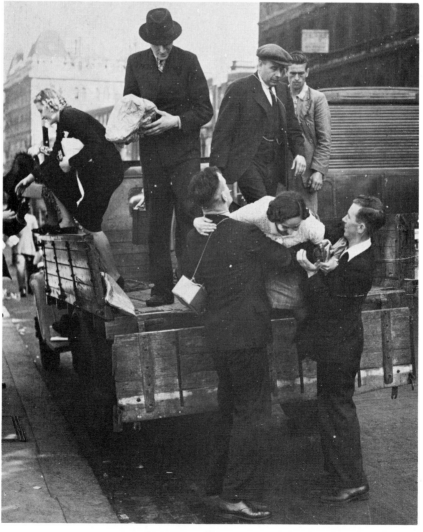

Opposite:
If in doubt, have a go – two Peckham air-raid wardens demonstrate their faith in improvisation.

WOMEN'S WORK

Patronising attitudes towards the 'frail sex' had no logical place in wartime. In the Great War of 1914-18 the total of working women had risen to some 7,500,000; after it, women had secured the vote. In this war their effort was to prepare the way for much broader social freedoms. Against such a background the War Cabinet could safely, in December 1941, introduce conscription for single women between 20 and 30; when called up, they had the option of going into industry or the auxiliary services.

The confrontation of a female war worker and her alloted machine was a situation dear to comedians and songwriters. One affectionate verse went like this:

She's the girl that makes the thing that drills the hole that holds the spring
That drives the rod that turns the knob that works the thingumebob.
She's the girl that makes the thing that holds the oil that oils the ring
That makes the shank that moves the crank that works the thingumebob.
It's a ticklish sort of job,
Making a thingumebob,
Especially when you don't know what it's for!
But it's the girl that makes the thing that drills the hole that holds the spring
That works the thingumebob that makes the engines roar.
And it's the girl that makes the thing that holds the oil that oils the ring
That works the thingumebob THAT'S GOING TO WIN THE WAR.

WOMEN OF BRITAIN
COME INTO THE FACTORIES

Mothers eager for war work demand adequate nursery facilities for their children.

Overleaf:
Girls in the Wheel Department of a Clapham bicycle factory stand to in their regulation tin helmets.

Women Fire Guards practise their new art.

Driving a tractor in the
harvest of 1943.

The Women's Land Army, formed in 1939 with a thousand volunteers, had swelled in two years to some twenty thousand, plus those
who then joined through conscription. Threshing was the usual job,
though others did horticultural or forestry work, and about a thousand
became rat catchers. Minimum pay was £2 8s a week, with seven days
leave a year.

Land Girls in a 1939 parade
of National Service
volunteers that was
reviewed by the King and
Queen.

Wye College students from
the Horticultural section
sow potatoes.

Land Girls at work in their
uniform green jerseys and
brown breeches.

THE NEW DEFENDERS

Women who opted for the auxiliary services generally found themselves in the WAAF, the ATS or the WRNS; duties were for the most part clerical but there were various 'action' jobs on, for example, searchlight and anti-aircraft batteries. Others worked as ferry pilots in the Air Transport Auxiliary, delivering warplanes from the factories.

Women in uniform at a Royal Observer Corps Centre, where the course of every aircraft, both friendly and otherwise, was plotted.

Overleaf, above:
Women of the Observer Corps at their post in the Eastern Counties.
Below:
Wrens on harbour boat-crew duty swab down the decks.

Recruiting poster for the WAAF. A correspondent who joined the WAAF in 43 recalls her first days of training: 'As we were herded from hut to hut we were encouraged by our officers and NCOs to sing *You are my Sunshine*. Hundreds of very young, very homesick, very cold and very miserable girls sang this song lustily.'

Left:
Voluntary Civil Defence workers get to grips with a rifle.

WRNS poster. For every 'home' job filled, a man could be freed for convoy and combat work.

HEROINES ALL

In the Phoney War period of 1939-40 unofficial groups of fighting women were formed with rather self-conscious titles like the Women's Amazon Defence Corps. By 1945 all need for fantasy names was gone, buried under the incalculable weight of women's wartime achievements.

A bus conductress-turned-farmhand.

A housewife/ferry pilot.

'THAT LOVELY WEEKEND'

For almost six years millions of couples spent long periods apart. Leave-time was wonderful but forever too short. In the words of the song:

Those two days of heaven you helped me to spend,
The thrill of your kiss as you stepped off the train,
The smile in your eyes like the sun after rain . . .

'Then breakfast next morning, just we two alone . . .'
(*That Lovely Weekend*)

'You had to go, the time was so short,
We both had so much to say,
Your kit to be packed, the train to be caught . . .'
(*That Lovely Weekend*)

DANCING THROUGH

aced with the nightly hundreds, all eager to be cheerful, band-leaders and vocalists lost no time in urging:

Everybody do the 'Blackout Stroll'
Laugh and drive your cares right up the pole.

Then the lights went out while everyone changed partners.

Catching the jitterbug. This craze began early in the war, then accelerated when the GIs arrived. In November 1939 some 1,4 fans crowded the Paramount, Tottenham Court Road for a 'Jitterbug Marathon'.

Jitterbug champions on display. Many dance halls were frightened by the jitterbug and barred it for as long as they could, but usually the public got what it wanted.

DANCING PARTNERS

Even if army boots were not ideal for dancing, the pretty partners made it a night to remember.

Open-air quick-stepping 'neath the balloon; Plymouth Hoe, July 1941.

Demonstrators launch the Kangaroo Hop, a novelty dance of 1941. Australians present were reported to have voted it 'dinkum'. Note also the AMOUR dress on the left of the photo – a brave confection for the first coupon winter.

THE DANCE BANDS

Some bands are remembered along with a place – if you say Lou Preager it is hard not to add 'at the Hammersmith Palais.' Among the radio regulars were Geraldo, Victor Silvester, Harry Roy, Billy Cotton, Mantovani, Henry Hall, Jack Payne, Ambrose, Joe Loss; many also packed up their trumpets and trombones and toured overseas with ENSA.

Ivy Benson leads her all-girl orchestra at a 1942 Halloween party.

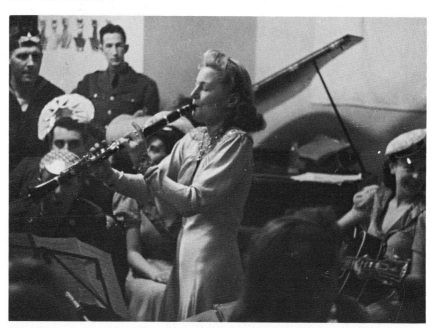

'THE DRUMS OF WAR, beating out their deafening discords, can never hope to supplant the insistent magic of music . . .' (from the cover of a songs album, published in 1940)

Harry Roy and his band in an Art Deco setting.

Henry Hall and vocalist
in a wartime dance hall.

Pre-war restraint from
Billy Cotton, at his
slimmest, and the band.

'BLESS 'EM ALL!'

V for Victory and plenty of beer. How about cigarettes? This notice doesn't say, but shortages there were – and felt deeply enough to be celebrated in song. One version, sung to the tune of *You are my Sunshine*, went: 'You are my sunshine, My double woodbine, My box of matches My Craven A.'

A round of '301' with the neighbours. Owning a dartboard saved stumbling about in the blackout or using up petrol coupons, and stay-at-home entertainments grew more popular.

Opposite, above: A leave-time sing-song round the piano. Back in Blighty there was time to laugh at the hardships of war, after all: 'Nobody knows what a twirp you've been. So cheer up, my lads, Bless 'em all!'
Below: Sailors to the fore – a bar scene in Liverpool, 1940.

FAR FROM HOME

The deprivations of war encouraged an element of fantasy, too; this may account for a somewhat surreal song called *Hugging and Chalking* which, a correspondent remembers, was about a 'chap who had this big girl friend, and when he hugged her, he had to make a chalk mark to see how far he'd got. It went something like this:

One day I was hugging and chalking . . .
When I met another fellow with some chalk in his hand,
Coming around the other way, over the mountain,
Coming around the other way.'

Satin dolls – with the added allure of tattooed arms and string suspenders.

December 1942: El Alamein has been won and Rommel driven back to Tunisia; an armoured car crew in the desert listens to a Christmas Day broadcast.

Opposite:
Christmas toasts on board a minesweeper; inset are the faces of wartime stars George Formby, Arthur Askey and Gracie Fields (in Italy); and the crew of an AA battery in Cyprus, tuning in to hear the latest from home.

THE SAGA OF LILLI MARLENE

Afrika Korps fans of Lilli Marlene en route to the lines at El Alamein.

Lilli Marlene was the song that both sides loved to sing. It was first recorded in 1939 by Lale Andersen in Germany where, bearing the unappetising title *Song of a Young Sentry*, it sold barely 700 copies and seemed set for the graveyard. Then, in 1941, Germany invaded Yugoslavia, and Belgrade Radio was taken over by a propaganda unit answerable to Dr Goebbels. Needing German songs but finding only Serbo-Croatian material in the Belgrade archives, the unit appealed to Vienna Radio who sent along a batch of old German records; among them was *Lilli Marlene*, as it soon came to be known.

This time it caught on, especially with Rommel's Afrika Korps who were well within range of the powerful Belgrade transmitter. So too, of course, were the men of the Allied Eighth Army; they also liked it and began to produce a barrage of parodies and bawdy versions. Eventually an uneasy British Government decided to commission Tommy Connor, the songwriter, to write a 'straight' English-language version. This was first recorded by Anne Shelton and became another hit. Elsewhere, Marlene Dietrich recorded her version in the USA, and in Italy it was sung by operatic tenors to Mussolini's reluctant troops. Within months the 'Lamplight Girl' was a worldwide favourite.

Anne Shelton, who first recorded Tommy Connor's version of the song. Right: Marlene Dietrich, who brought out another, throatier recording.

Infantry and tankmen of the Eighth Army – who became Lilli's newest admirers.

Sheet music cover of the German song, originally known as the *Song of a Young Sentry*.

FIGHTING SONGS

Songs inspired by particular campaigns had a habit of soon losing their point, and rarely achieved lasting popularity; such was the fate of that vanished desert song *Where do we go from here, Now that we've captured Bardia?* However, a few songs based on more generally familiar themes became hits – songs such as *Comin' in on a Wing and a Prayer* which told the story of 'J for Jimmy and all the gallant crew' limping home from a raid with one engine gone.

Bombing up a Lancaster, Britain's most successful bomber in the war. In one of the many 'variant' songs of the war, the word 'Bomber' was substituted for 'Bonny', thus *Bring back my Bomber to Me.*

Patriotic pyjamas of pale blue, piped in navy and embroidered with an Air Force emblem (8 coupons).

Held together by string and a prayer? These Swordfish biplanes, seen in their D-Day markings, were in reality much tougher than they may seem to us today, 30 years later.

THE WAR AT SEA

One of the most arduous campaigns of the war was the Battle of the Atlantic fought between the Allied convoys, bringing essential supplies to Britain and Russia, and the deadly U-boats of Admiral Dönitz. It was out of the naval war that another 'action' song was born, *Praise the Lord and Pass the Ammunition*: this song concerned a ship's chaplain who, stopped in mid-service by an attack, ran to help load the guns.

An ocean convoy of 1941 creeps towards its destination port.

Men from the frigates of an Atlantic convoy with their Jolly Roger showing five U-boats sunk.

THE GI'S ARE HERE

GIs, so named after the words 'Government Issue' which appeared on their equipment, began to arrive early in 1942. On 26 January, 2,900 men were disembarked at Belfast and they and succeeding waves were soon dispersed all over Britain. At first the comparative, PX-induced ease of their life tended to arouse resentment, provoking the native saying that GIs were 'overpaid, oversexed and over here'. But their generosity and extrovert ways soon won them friends enough and they came to add a fresh and largely welcome dimension to the wartime scene.

The first contingent of the American Expeditionary Force marches from the quay in Belfast.

GIs in a pub shortly before D-Day.

Opposite:
Tommy Atkins and his new friend.

RAINBOW CORNER

Largest of the American Red Cross clubs in London was Rainbow Corner, in Coventry Street, near Piccadilly Circus. To it streamed men who, speaking with the accents of Movieland, brought to a glamour-starved Britain an air of romance as well as the harder currency of cigarettes, candy and nylons. Lots of girls found them good company. After the war some eighty thousand GI brides went off to a new life in the USA.

Servicemen gather outside Rainbow Corner, the American Red Cross club near Piccadilly Circus.

Hand in hand at a wartime dance hall.

Low lights on the dance floor.

Opposite:
A glance exchanged in the coffee shop at Rainbow Corner.

MOVIE ROMANTICS

Cinemas were closed for a short while, along with other places of entertainment, at the beginning of the war; when they re-opened they became treasured havens of escape. Favourite films included *The Wizard of Oz*, the Hope-Crosby *Road* films and, above all others, *Gone with the Wind*; to see it people queued unmoving through air raids, and in the West End of London it ran from mid-1940 until D-Day.

Veronica Lake, whose shoulder-length hairstyle was much copied. This greatly alarmed the Ministry of Labour as come-hither locks hovered dangerously close to factory machines.

Joan Crawford, elegant as a heroine of the French Resistance in *Mademoiselle France*.

Clark Gable and Vivien
~~~gh in *Gone with the Wind*,~~~
~~~e~~~ film industry's greatest
wartime blockbuster.

Britain's own glamour
queen, Margaret
Lockwood, in *The Wicked
Lady*.

D-DAY

The invasion of Europe, for which a vast Allied force had been secretly built up 'somewhere in England', came on 6 June 1944. The British Second Army and the US First Army gained essential footholds on the beaches of Normandy between Cherbourg and Le Havre, from where the Allies were eventually able to fan out across France and chase the Germans back across the Rhine. As they rested between fights, they were treated by radio to some of the war's most empty-headed songs, a leading contender being the (to some) infuriatingly catchy *Mairzy Doats and Dozy Doats*.

A Chelsea Pensioner shares the news of the invasion with passers-by.

D-Day on an American beach in Normandy.

Opposite:
A GI waves goodbye to his pinups before leaving for Normandy.

WILL IT EVER END?

Back home the rigours of war persisted. V-1 and V-2 rocket attacks laid siege to the south; the death-toll went on growing and the war entered its sixth year.

A V-1 rocket explodes, silhouetting one of the battery of AA guns which had shot it down.

July 1944, Dover: people take shelter in the caves.

September 1944, Lewisham: bombed-out Londoners are interviewed in a requisitioned dance hall.

VE DAY AND AFTER

Germany surrendered on 7 May 1945. Next day was VE Day (Victory in Europe): in the afternoon Churchill broadcast to the nation and that night, at last, wishes came true and the lights went up in London. Three months later came Japan's capitulation, marked by VJ Day. Long years of austerity lay ahead but these were temporarily ignored in a great splurge of thanksgiving and celebration. *Don't Fence Me In* was a hit song of the day, its title and jumpy tempo encapsulating the way people felt about being free.

Overleaf, top left:
Flag-seller in Oxford Street.
Below left:
Cyclist and baby-trailer near Buckingham Palace.

Top right:
Newspaper headlines for 8 May 1945.

Below right:
Canadian soldiers, a British sailor and Hertfordshire Land Girls in St James's Park.
Far right:
In Trafalgar Square the pigeons, displaced by victory crowds, shift their perch to the base of Nelson's Column.

Below:
Dancing in The Street – Fleet Street, that is.

pyramid of merrymakers in Parliament Square.

The war lord, wreathed in a frame of flowers.

Daily Mail

NO. 15,290   ONE PENNY   FOR KING AND EMPIRE   TUESDAY, MAY 8, 1945

VICTORY EDITION

TUESday FIELD-DAY

3-POWER ANNOUNCEMENT TO-DAY; BUT BRITAIN KNEW LAST NIGHT

VE-DAY—IT'S ALL OVER

All quiet till 9 p.m.—then the London crowds went mad in the West End

By Day ↑
↓ By Night

PM put off the big speech

UNTIL TO-DAY

By WILSON BROADBENT, Diplomatic Correspondent

GERMANY surrendered unconditionally to the Allies yesterday. But there will be no official announcement of victory until 3 p.m. to-day officially described as VE-Day—when Mr. Churchill will give the news to the world.

CZECHS TOLD TO 'SMASH GERMANS'

TARAKAN NEARLY CUT IN TWO

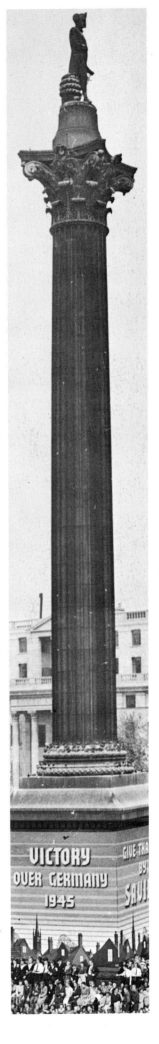

VICTORY OVER GERMANY 1945

GIVE THA...
BY...
SAVI...

Queuing for kisses after
the Victory parade.

Newspaper workers dance
to the accordion man.

Opposite:
The Royal coach returns
from a Thanksgiving
Service at St Paul's.

OUR STREET PARTY

There was a lot of celebrating to be done – not just on VE Day or VJ Day but also when the fighting men came home on leave or got their demob. At various times streets that once were blacked out and bleak turned red, white and blue with flags and bunting; children at tea parties ate jellies and jam tarts until they turned green; there were bonfire parties and fancy-dress parades. And in the evenings the old songs of the blackout were sung with gusto and even, possibly, the first twinges of nostalgia:

Joe brought his concertina, and Nobby brought the beer,
And all the little nippers swung upon the chandelier!
A blackout warden passin' yelled, Ma, pull down that blind,
Just look at what you're showin', and we shouted, 'Never mind.' OOOH!
Knees up, Mother Brown! Well, Knees up, Mother Brown, etc.

Out come the flags and a welcome placard for Bill, Tom, George, Bob, George and Joe.

WELCOME HOME

Bonfire party in Havering Street, Stepney.

A children's feast to celebrate VE Day.

ACKNOWLEDGEMENTS

The author of *The Home Front in Pictures* is grateful for the help of a number of published sources which provided much valuable information about the war period, most notably *How We Lived Then*, by Norman Longmate (Hutchinson/ Arrow); *The People's War*, by Angus Calder (Cape/Panther); *The Phoney War on the Western Front*, by E. S. Turner (Michael Joseph); *British Women in War*, by Peggy Scott (Hutchinson); *The Theatre at War*, by Basil Dean (Harrap); *Why Britain is at War*, by Harold Nicolson (Penguin), and *War Begins at Home*, a Mass Observation survey by Madge & Harrison (Chatto & Windus). He also acknowledges the helpful contributions of all who responded to his appeals in the press and on radio for memories connected with particular songs; they are too numerous to list in full but special thanks go to Mr H. Coverley of Woodgreen, Hampshire; Mrs H. Frith, Tadcaster, Yorkshire; Mrs C Gittins, Abingdon, Oxfordshire; Mr M. Jacobs, Brighton, Sussex; Mrs P. Martin, formerly of Deptford, Kent; Mrs B. Meredith, Birchington, Kent; Mrs M. Rayner, Wickford, Essex; and Mrs. M Wishart, Rome, Italy.

The author and publishers are also grateful to the following organizations for their help in providing photographs:

Camera Press 6T, 9, 12B, 14T, 15, 47, 63BR, 86, 91R.
Central Press 17B, 19TL, TR, 32BC, 42TR, 59B, 95T.
Conway Picture Library 12TL, TR, 28T, 67B, 68B, 72B.
Fox Photos 10BR, 11T, 14BL, BC, 16, 17T, 19B, 20, 25BL, 38, 40B, 41B, 43BR, 48, 49T, 50, 54, 56BL, 57, 69B, 88T, 90B.
Imperial War Museum 10BL, 23B, 27, 28B, 29, 32T, 40C, 43T, 46T, 51BR, 52BL, 53T, BL, 58, 63BL, 64B, 74B, 75BR, 76, 77B, 78T, 79T, 81B, 87B.
Interfoto, Munich 77BR.
Kobal Collection 84, 85.
Mansell Collection 34T, 40T, 52BR, 63T, 64T, 81T.
National Maritime Museum 78BR.
Pictorial Press 30T, 39B, 42B, 65T.
Popperfoto 7T, 14BR, 22B, 26, 30B, 33T, 35B, 36B, 42TL, 43BL, 46BR, 51BL, 52T, 66, 67T, 73T, 74T, 79B, 89, 90T, 91T, B, 92, 93, 94, 95B.
Radio Times Hulton Picture Library 7B, 8, 10T, 11B, 13, 18, 21, 22T, 23T, 24, 25T, BR, 31, 32BL, BR, 33B, 35T, 36T, 37, 39T, 41T, 44, 45, 49B, 51T, 53BR, 55, 56T, BR, 59T, 60, 61, 62, 63B, 65BL, 68T, BL, 69T, 70, 71, 72T, 73B, 75 (except BR), 77TL, TR, 78BL, 82, 83, 87T, 88C, B.
WVS/Fox Photos 43C.

THERE'LL ALWAYS BE AN ENGLAND

Words and music by Ross Parker and Hugh Charles

98

REFRAIN

100

white and blue, What does it mean to you? Sure-ly you're proud, shout it a loud, Britens a-wake The

Em-pire too, we can de-pend on you, Freedom remains these are the chains, nothing can break, ___ There'll

al-ways be an Eng-land And Eng-land shall be free, If Eng-land means as

much to you As Eng-land means ___ to me. ___

I'LL BE SEEING YOU

Words by Irving Kahl   Music by Sammy Fain

LORDS OF THE AIR

Words and music by Michael North and Davy Burnaby

106

this be our new bat-tle-cry, "Bri-tan-nia rules the air."
on, fly on to vic-to-ry, "Bri-tan-nia rules the air."

REFRAIN

Eng-land our is-land home,— Land of the free,—

Eng-land un-con-quered yet — O'er land and

LET THE PEOPLE SING

Words by Frank Eyton and Ian Grant   Music by Noel Gay

VERSE

LET THE PEO-PLE SING   Sing like an-y-thing   An-y sort of song they choose

LET THE PEO-PLE SING   Let the wel-kin ring   An-y-thing to kill the blues

Find a mer-ry song to   cheer them   Tell them that I long to

hear them   When things all go wrong   You will find a song   Wel-come as a breath of

spring   There-fore LET THE PEO-PLE   SING.   SING.

I'LL PRAY FOR YOU

Words and music by Roy King and Stanley Hill

VERSE

WE'LL MEET AGAIN

Words and music by Ross Parker and Hugh Charles

Moderato espressivo

Let's say good-bye with a smile dear,— Just for a while dear,— We must part,
Af-ter the rain comes the rain-bow,— You'll see the rain go,— Nev-er fear,

Don't let the part-ing up-set you,— I'll not for-get you sweet-heart.
We two can wait for to-mor-row,— Good-bye to sor-row my dear.

REFRAIN

WE'LL MEET A-GAIN don't know where, Don't know when, But I know we'll meet a-

113

SOMEWHERE IN FRANCE WITH YOU

Moderately *(Smoothly)*

Words and music by Michael Carr

CHORUS

There are two eyes, such blue eyes, a smil-ing at me Yet they're lone - ly as on - ly a wom-an's can be For I see all her thoughts are some — where, Some-where in France with you. While she's talk - ing, she's talk - ing of no - one but

116

KISS ME GOODNIGHT, SERGEANT MAJOR

Words and music by Art Noel and Don Pelosi

Pri-vate Jones came in one night Full of cheer and ve-ry bright

He'd been out all day up-on the spree _____ He bumped in-to Ser-geant Smeck

Put his arms a-round his neck And in his ear he whis-pered ten-der-ly. _____

NURSIE! NURSIE!

Words and music by Art Noei and Don Pelosi

Allegro moderato

Ev-'ry day in the park when the troops are marching by, There's a nurse, what a nurse, and she catch-es ev-'ry eye; What a style, what a smile, can you won-der why they fall, From the Colonel to the Pri-vate, you'll hear the ar-my call—

IN THE QUARTERMASTER'S STORES (MY EYES ARE DIM, I CANNOT SEE)

Words and music adapted by Elton Box, Desmond Cox and Bert Reed

126

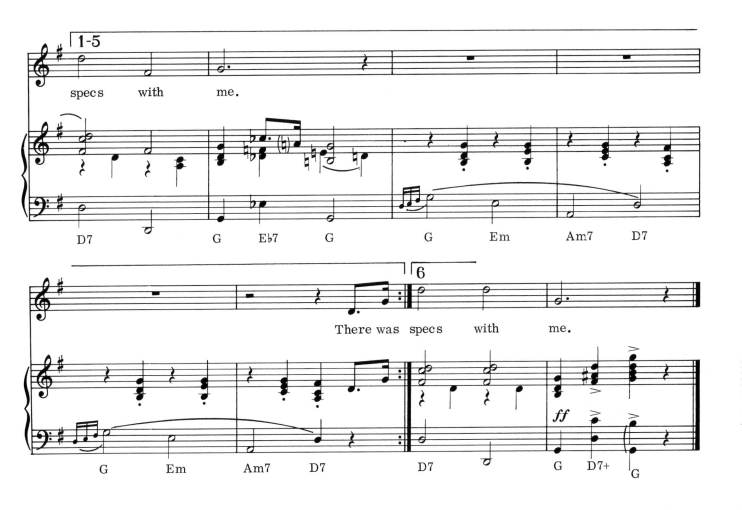

2. There was bread, bread
Just like lumps of lead,
In the stores, in the stores,
There were buns, buns
Bullets for the guns,
In the quartermaster's stores.
My eyes are dim, I cannot see, *etc.*

3. There was mice, mice
Eating up the rice
In the stores, in the stores
There were rats, rats
Big as blooming cats
In the quartermaster's stores.
My eyes are dim, I cannot see, *etc.*

4. There was meat, meat
Meat you couldn't eat
In the stores, in the stores,
There were eggs, eggs
Nearly growing legs
In the quartermaster's stores.
My eyes are dim, I cannot see, *etc.*

5. There is beer, beer
Beer you can't get near
In the stores, in the stores,
There is rum, rum
For the General's tum
In the quartermaster's stores.
My eyes are dim, I cannot see, *etc.*

6. There was cake, cake
Cake you couldn't break
In the stores, in the stores,
There were flies, flies
Feeding on the pies
In the quartermaster's stores.
My eyes are dim, I cannot see, *etc.*

(We're Gonna Hang Out)
THE WASHING ON THE SIEGFRIED LINE

Words and music by Jimmy Kennedy and Michael Carr

RUN, RABBIT, RUN!

Words by Noel Gay and Ralph Butler   Music by Noel Gay

132

A NIGHTINGALE SANG IN BERKELEY SQUARE

Words by Eric Maschwitz   Music by Manning Sherwin

134

That cer-tain night, the night we met, there was mag-ic a-broad in the air There were
strange it was, how sweet and strange, there was nev-er a dream to com-pare With that

an-gels din-ing at the Ritz, And a night-in-gale sang in *Ber———k'ley
ha-zy, cra-zy night we met, When a night-in-gale sang in Ber———k'ley

Square.
Square.

I may be right, I may be wrong, but I'm
This heart of mine, beat loud and fast, like a

per-fect-ly will-ing to swear, That when you turn'd and smil'd at me, A
mer-ry-go-round in a fair, For we were danc-ing cheek to cheek, And a

night-in-gale sang in Ber———k'ley Square.
night-in-gale sang in Ber———k'ley Square.

MISTER BROWN OF LONDON TOWN

Words and music by Reginald Arkell and Noel Gay

ROLL OUT THE BARREL (Beer Barrel Polka)

Words and music by Lew Brown, Wladimir A. Timm and Jaromir Vejvoda

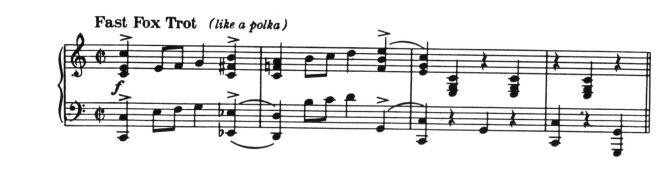

139

YOU ARE MY SUNSHINE

Words and music by Jimmy Davis and Charles Mitchell

143

CHORUS

HEY! LITTLE HEN

Words and music by Ralph Butler and Noel Gay

146

I'VE GOT SIXPENCE (AS I GO ROLLING HOME)

Words and music by Elton Box, Desmond Cox and Laurence T. Hall

Moderato

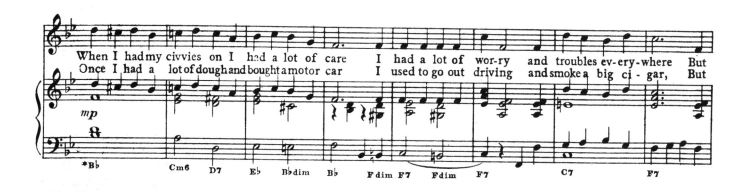

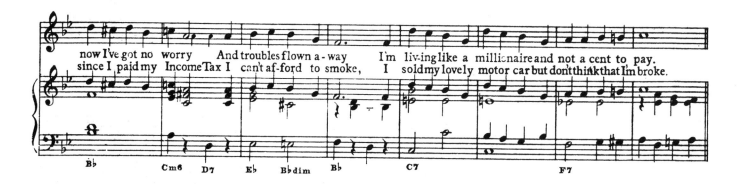

DER FUEHRER'S FACE

Words and music by Oliver Wallace

A la "Dutch Band"

Ven der Fueh - rer says, "Ve iss der Mas - ter
Goeb - bels says, "Ve own der Vorld und

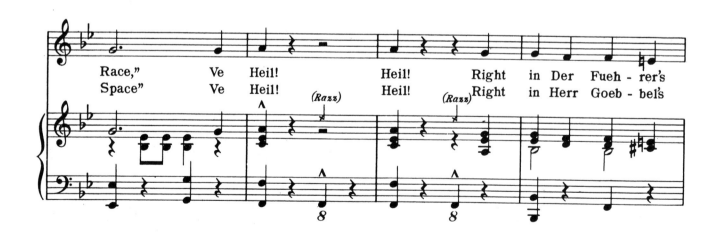

Race," Ve Heil! (Razz) Heil! (Razz) Right in Der Fueh - rer's
Space" Ve Heil! Heil! Right in Herr Goeb - bel's

150

Iss ve not der Su - per - men? Ar - yan pure, Su - per - men?

Ya! ve iss der Su - per - men, Su - per, Du - per, Su - per - men!

Iss der nut - sy land so goot, Vould you leave it if you could?

Ya! dis nut - sy land is goot, Ve vould leave it if ve could!

(There'll Be Blue Birds Over) THE WHITE CLIFFS OF DOVER

Words by Nat Burton   Music by Walter Kent
Additional Lyrics by D. Elvins

153

THAT LOVELY WEEKEND

Words and music by Moira and Ted Heath

Moderato (*with feeling*)

My darling, here's my letter, I'm writing through my tears, A few sweet words to thank you for lovely sou-ven-irs,

Mem-o-ries you gave me still ech-o in my heart, I'll dream of them while we're a - part.

I haven't said thanks for that lovely week-end, Those two days of hea-ven you helped me to spend, The

thrill of your kiss as you stepped off the train, The smile in your eyes like the sun af-ter rain. To

155

mark the oc-ca-sion we went out to dine, Re-member the laughter, the music the wine; That drive in the tax - i when

midnight had flown, Then breakfast next morning, just we two a - lone. You had to go, the time was so short, We

both had so much to say;— Your kit to be packed, the train to be caught, Sor-ry I cried but I

just felt that way. And now you have gone, dear, this letter I pen; My heart travels with you till we meet a-gain. Keep

smiling, my darling, and someday we'll spend A lifetime as sweet as that love-ly weekend. I love-ly weekend.

YOURS

Words by Jack Sherr   Music by Gonzalo Roig

I DON'T WANT TO
SET THE WORLD ON FIRE

Words and music by Eddie Seiler, Sol Marcus, Bennie Benjemen and Eddie Durham

159

LILLI MARLENE

Words and music by Hans Leip, Norbert Schultz and Tommie Connor

Un-der neath the lan-tern by the bar-rack gate, Dar-ling I re-mem-ber the way you used to wait;'Twas
Time would come for roll call, time for us to part, Dar-ling I'd caress you and press you to my heart; And

There that you whis-pered ten-der-ly, That you lov'd me, You'd al-ways be,
There 'neath that far off lan-tern light, I'd hold you tight, We'd kiss "Good-night;" My Lil-li of the

lamp-light, My own LIL-LI MAR-LENE.

I'M THINKING TONIGHT OF MY BLUE EYES

Words and music by A. P. Carter

CHORUS

BLESS 'EM ALL

Words and music by Jimmy Hughes and Frank Lake

Brightly

1. They say there's a troop-ship just leav-ing Bom-bay,
2. They say, if you work hard you'll get bet-ter pay,
3. They say that the Ser-geant's a ve-ry nice chap,
4. They say that the Cor-p'ral will help you a-long,

Bound for Old Bligh-ty shore,____ Heav-i-ly la-den with time ex-pired men, Bound for the
We've heard it all be-fore,____ Clean up your but-tons and pol-ish your boots, Scrub out the
Oh! what a tale to tell!____ Ask him for leave on a Sat-ur-day night He'll pay your
Oh! what an aw-ful crime,____ Lend him your ra-zor to clean up his chin, He'll bring it

land they a-dore.____ There's man-y an air-man just finishing his time, There's man-y a twirp signing
bar-rack room floor.____ There's man-y a rook-ie has tak-en it in, Hook line and sink-er an'
fare home as well.____ There's man-y an air-man has blight-ed his life, Thro' writ-ing rude words on the
back ev-'ry time.____ There's man-y a rook-ie has fell in the mud, Thro' leav-ing his horse in the

on,____ You'll get no pro-mo-tion this side of the o-cean, So cheer up, my lads, Bless 'em all!
all,____ You'll get no pro-mo-tion this side of the o-cean, So cheer up, my lads, Bless 'em all!____
wall,____ You'll get no pro-mo-tion this side of the o-cean, So cheer up, my lads, Bless 'em all!____
stall,____ You'll get no pro-mo-tion this side of the o-cean, So cheer up, my lads, Bless 'em all!____

165

CLEANIN' MY RIFLE
(AND DREAMIN' OF YOU)

Words and music by Allie Wrubel

Moderato

VERSE

The boys were hang-in' 'round camp that night, Won-d'rin' what to-mor-row'd bring, A

ban - jo chord came thru the blue, And I heard some-bod-y sing:

CHORUS

Lit - tle bit lone - some, _____ lit - tle bit blue, _____

MAIRZY DOATS AND DOZY DOATS
(Mares Eat Oats and Does Eat Oats)

Words and music by Milton Drake, Al Hoffman and Jerry Livingston

COMIN' IN ON A WING AND A PRAYER

Words by Harold Adamson   Revised words by Frederick Day   Music by Jimmy McHugh

1. O - ver the dim lit flare path an anx-ious si - lence
2. Lis - ten-ing-watch-ing - hop-ing - was all that we could

reigned,   Scan-ning the blue ho - ri - zon our anx-ious eyes were
do,   Wait-ing for J. for Jim-my and all the gal - lant

strained. The ra - di - o sets were hum-ming, they wait - ed for a
crew.   Then o - ver our long—ing vis - ion a dim grey shad -ow

174

I'M GONNA GET LIT-UP

Words and music by Hubert Gregg

When the na-tions lose their war-sense, and the world gets back its horse-sense, What a day for cel-e-bra-tion that will be. When some-bo-dy shouts "The fight's up!" and "It's time to put the lights up!" Then the first thing to be lit-up will be me.

more, much more, And be-fore the par-ty's played out, they will fetch the Fire Bri-gade out To the
canned, canned, canned, Thro' our Gins and An-go-stu-ras, we'll see lit-tle pale pink Fueh-rers, Hi de

F E7 Am E7 Am F Cdim C Cdim C A7 Ab A7

1 **2**

lit-test-up-pest scene you ev-er saw._____ I'm going to get saw._____
Heil-ing from the Cir-cus to the Strand._____ I'm going to get Strand._____

D7 G7 F G7 C C7 Cdim Fm6 C G7 C C7 Cdim Fm6 C

ADDITIONAL CHORUSES

3.
A regular flare-up when they light Trafalgar Square up,
A regular sight to open Nelson's other eye,
Through the day and through the night,
Signal beacons they will light,
"England this day expects the nation to be tight."
They'll have to stop traffic when they light Trafalgar Square up,
And down the rocky road to Westminster we'll reel, reel, reel,
What a shindy we will kick up,
Old Big Ben will chime a hiccup,
To epitomise the sentiments we feel.

4.
I'm going to get unsedately so serenely stinking
I'm going to get stinking as I've never been before,
When the dogs have had their day,
And the fight has had its fray,
We'll all be swapping battle-dress for bottle dress that day.
I'm going to get positively permanently pie-eyed,
The day we finally exterminate the Huns, Huns, Huns,
There'll be joy and there'll be laughter,
And there'll be no Morning After,
For we'll all be drunk for muns and muns and muns.

PRAISE THE LORD AND PASS THE AMMUNITION

Words and music by Frank Loesser

Martial

Down went the gun-ner, a bul-let was his fate;

Down went the gun-ner, and then the gun-ner's mate. Up jumped the sky pi-lot,

gave the boys a look And manned the gun him-self as he laid a-side The Book, shout-ing:

180

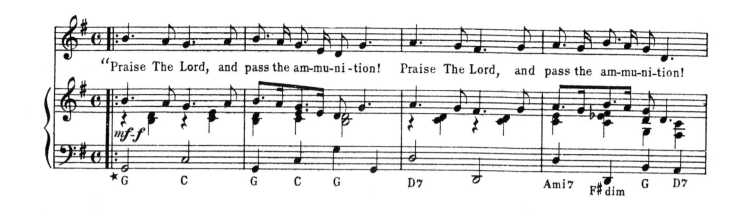

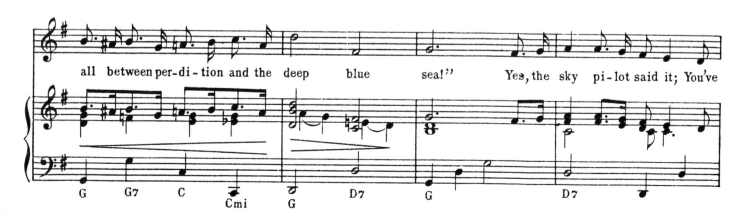

got to give him cred-it, for a son-of-a-gun of a gun-ner was he. Shout-ing:

G   B7   Emi   A7   A9   A7   D7   C   D7

"Praise The Lord, we're on a might-y mis-sion! All a-board! We're not a-go-in' fish-in',

G   C   G   C   G   D7   Ami7   F#dim   G   D7

|1 |2

Praise The Lord, and pass the am-mu-ni-tion and we'll all stay free." free."

G   C   G   G7   C   Cmi   G   D7   G C#dim Ami7 D7   G   FINE

New from Music Sales - the one-and only, ultimate busker book! It's *the* book to take to a party... to a gig... on your holiday... or to that famous desert island!

It's packed with literally hundreds and hundreds of the best-loved songs of all time... from vintage standards of the 30s right through to the latest pop hits.

"The Suitcase Book"!

While compiling this huge book, editor/arranger Peter Lavender kept all the artwork in a huge suitcase! But now that it's printed, this new mega-bumper busker book is a lot easier to carry around!

Surprisingly portable, in fact, at the usual songbook size of 12" x 9"... with some 656 pages!

As well as the 1,001 songs, the book includes a handy A-Z alphabetical title index *and* a classified index, too.